The

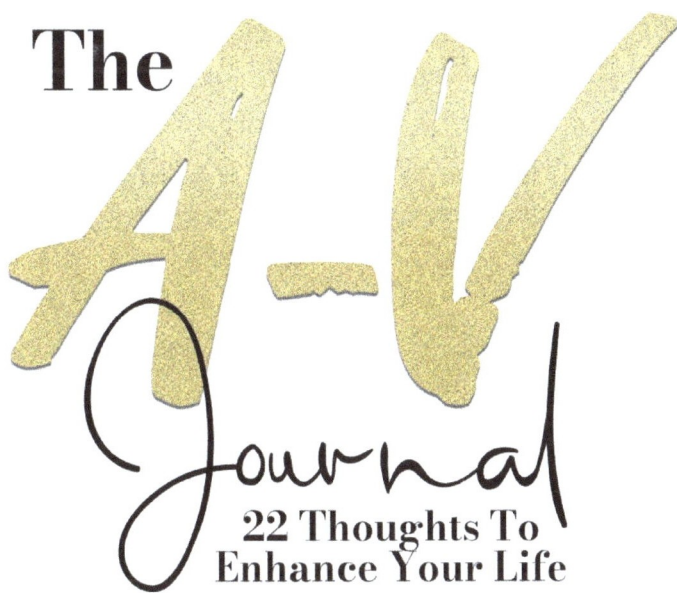

22 Thoughts To
Enhance Your Life

Presented by
The V List Podcast
VICTORIA NJIDEKA

Published Services by: Pen Legacy Publishing
Cover by: Christian Cuan
Edited by: Victoria Njideka
Interior Design & Formatted by Victoria Njideka & Tamika Hall
Photography By: Ashleigh Bing Photography

Library of Congress Cataloging – in- Publication Data has been applied for.

ISBN: 979-8-9852065-7-9

PRINTED IN THE UNITED STATES OF AMERICA.

First Edition

Table of Contents

Introduction

Welcome to the V List! If you are using this journal, then you are officially a part of the list! This journal is based on the A-V series from my podcast where I shared motivational content to help you improve your emotional intelligence and overall life. It is meant to be inspiring, educational, and enlightening. Because I believe that we are spiritual beings having a human experience, I also utilize scripture to help provide a spiritual context to the topics being discussed. Regardless of your belief system, scripture has always been useful and applicable daily living and provides me with encouragement along the way. I love to refer to the Bible under the acronym:

Basic **I**nstructions **B**efore **L**eaving **E**arth.

My hope is that this journal (Vol 1) will help to increase your life with the topics that I feel are important to remember as a spiritual being from A-V!

How To Use This Journal

There are 22 entries in this journal for you to complete in either 22 days, 22 weeks, or 22 months! The decision is yours. Each entry will introduce the topic, provide you with a lesson or thought, provide you with references to do your own research, and finally a section for you to record your thoughts and action steps to follow. The journal begins at A and goes through to .... you guessed it, V! After all this is the V List!

-A-
ANXIETY

don't mean to be harsh but...anxiety is a liar. Just like fear. I'm not trying to be insensitive to those who have suffered or are suffering from sometimes crippling anxiety...but I want to let you know that you are being fooled, lied to, deceived! If there was someone that you had a close relationship with and you found out that they were lying to you constantly to keep you captive, would you still allow them in your space? NO! So do that with anxiety too!

Let's be clear about what's anxiety vs. your intuition trying to warn you about something. Everyone has intuition, some have more than others or are just more tapped in. Once you become aligned, you'll be able to listen to your intuition then you'll be able to decipher between intuition and that lying anxiety! Anxiety is tricky! It can show up as excitement, fear, nervousness, bubble guts, etc. One thing I would suggest is trying to look for clues. If your anxiety is your intuition trying to warn you then there will be clues or confirmations that confirm what you were feeling. These clues can be small, large, in your face, or subtle. It could be a song, a picture you see, a message you receive, a dream you have, all those things are clues. Again, you must be aligned to recognize the signs. But if you don't have any clues to prove your fear or you have tried to connect dots and nothing is connecting to confirm the fear, you're experiencing then more than likely it is just anxiety, lying to you again.

Let's confront it now. List the top three things that come to mind that give you anxiety.

My Top Anxiety Triggers are:

_____

_____

_____

Whenever these events occur that you listed above, does what you fear ever actually take place? If so, then that means there were warning signs that you ignored. But if not, I challenge you to start dismissing those anxious thoughts the next time you're triggered. And start to implement the strategies and instruction given to us

"Do not be anxious about anything, but in every situation, by prayer and petition, with thanksgiving, present your requests to God. And the peace of God which transcends all understanding will guard your hearts and your minds in Christ Jesus. Finally,

brothers and sisters, whatever is true, whatever is noble, whatever is right, whatever is pure, whatever is lovely, whatever is admirable- if anything is excellent or praiseworthy- think about such things!" Philippians 4:6-8 NIV

The scripture tells us what to do to combat anxiety.

First, pray and petition God, but do it with gratitude! It is quite rude to approach someone and ask for something and you never thanked them for the last blessing they gave you. Don't do God that way either!

After praying, God will grant you some peace and calm and you might be a little confused by it but hopefully, that is what you asked for when you prayed.

Next, it tells us what to fix our thoughts on instead of those anxiety triggers. Whatever you can think of that is true, all those good things that make you smile. It could be the ocean, cupcakes & rainbows, sunshine & beaches, people you love, your favorite food! Anything! As long as it's real, true, lovely, noble, etc.! Afterward hopefully your anxiety will start to subside.

I hope this helps!

Reflective Thoughts:

_____

_____

_____

_____

_____

_____

_____

_____

_____

_____

_____

_____

_____

_____

_____

_____

_____

_____

_____

_____

_____

-B-

BURNOUTS, BREAKS & BALANCE

I f you're experiencing burnout then that means you probably aren't balancing properly, and you need a break!! A part of this toxic #PressureCulture that we live in is glorifying being busy all the time. But that's a quick and easy way to burnout, and the bottom line is burnout isn't cute! The key to finding balance is prioritization. There are going to be some things that require a little more time, effort, and energy. So, it causes the scales of your life to become a bit imbalanced. You'll start to feel weighed down, heavy, tired, probably dragging a bit. This is an indicator that you need a break!

It is useless for you to work so hard from early morning until late at night, anxiously working for food to eat. God gives rest to his loved ones! -Psalms 127:2 NLT

All that hard work you're doing with no breaks or rest is all in vain! I believe in taking breaks and living a balanced life so that I do not experience burnout.

It's the break for me!!

Do this time allotment activity below to see how you are spending your time during the week. Start with 168 hrs. and subtract from there. This is an average of the time that you spend doing these activities during the week, so be as honest as possible. Whatever hours you have leftover is the time you can use to schedule breaks with! We have more time than we think. And no, it's not time that you need to sleep because that's already accounted for in the activity, but if you want to sleep with your extra time, do you! If you are out of time by the end of your week then it's time for some serious changes to be made.

Here's an example:

Where's My Break Activity?	Avg Hrs. (p/week)
Sleep	42
Exercise	4
Work	40
Commute	5
Caregiving (elder, pet, child)	2.5
Choring (Cooking, cleaning)	4
Other (misc. things you may do) podcasting, writing, etc.	15
Total Hours	107.5

168 - (Total Hours) =	55.5

After my time allotment to the obligations, I have I still had almost 56 hours left over.

Your Turn:

Where's My Break Activity?	Avg Hrs. (p/week)
Sleep	
Exercise	
Work	
Commute	
Caregiving (elder, pet, child)	
Choring (Cooking, cleaning)	
Other (misc. things you may do)	
Total Hours	

168 - (Total Hours) =	

Whenever you start to feel burnout, think about what you would rather be doing, then go do that! Use the space below to list out ways you can start to utilize the time you found, or journal about what all you have going on and start to prioritize, or you can just vent. It's your journal!

Reflective Thoughts:

_____

_____

_____

_____

_____

_____

_____

_____

_____

_____

_____

_____

_____

_____

_____

_____

_____

_____

-C-
COVERED

O ne of my favorite scriptures is **Psalms 91**. Take a moment to read that scripture in its entirety.

I like to think of this scripture as an insurance policy. The Lord is letting us know that regardless of what we go through or face we are covered. Being connected and aligned certainly has its benefits! We all need a covering of some sort, so I would encourage you to seek refuge in a source higher than yourself. Then take pride in the fact that you are covered!

I hope this serves as encouragement for you today.

List situations you feel protected & covered from:

1._____

2._____

3._____

4._____

5._____

6._____

7._____

Doesn't it feel good to feel protected! Be sure to express gratitude for these things today. Then pray for the guidance and protection for the areas in your life that you feel you need more protection in. Just know that once you ask you will probably get it.

Reflective Thoughts:

_____

_____

_____

_____

_____

_____

_____

_____

_____

_____

_____

_____

_____

_____

_____

_____

_____

_____

_____

-D-
DEBT

D ebt sucks! Even though most of us have it. Some more than others. I don't like it. I admittedly in the past have not been the best steward of my funds. Sorry God! However, I have gotten a lot better! And I'm improving day by day by starting with a budget. I used to hate budgeting, and I'm still not the best at it, because it shows me the ugly side of my finances, which is my debt. The bottom line is I like to spend money, but it isn't cute to be spending a bunch of money when I have a bunch of debt.

Also, get rid of the idea that you must be rich or poor to have a budget...you'll probably find that in order to become rich, though you NEED a budget.

The other thing about money and debt is it starts with your mindset. Yes, I know that sounds cliché' but it's sooo true. Until I started thinking differently about my relationship with money, I was still making very poor decisions with it. I also felt like I would always be in debt. But today I know that is a lie! I WILL be debt free!

My goal right now isn't so much to become rich(er) but mainly to eliminate my debt. I don't want to owe anyone anything! I want to be able to help others and be the lender, not the borrower!

Now since I'm NOT a financial professional or guru I won't tell you any "proven" methods...I'm only sharing what I have done to help me on my journey to become debt-free. Every journey starts with the first step...and the first step to getting out of debt is to face it! So, let's list out all of your debts.

The only debt I'm trying to owe is the debt of love to others.

"Let no debt remain outstanding, except the continuing debt to love one another, for whoever loves others has fulfilled the law." Romans 13:8 NIV

Activity

List out all your current debt. After looking at the total amount owed, the monthly payments and your monthly income then you can determine a strategy to begin paying off your debt. There are TONS of resources available for debt elimination. A simple google search can get you well on your way to being debt free. Something I like to do to get a hold on my debt is listing it all out. Start there.

Current Debt	Credit Limit	Current Balance	Minimum Payment	Due Date
Ex. American Express	$1000	$300	$40	6th of each month
		Total Debt =	Amount owed monthly =	

Now I want to share this decree over your finances that I've heard recited at a few churches I have attended over the past few years. Read this, print it out, recite it aloud!

"God, I thank you that I'm anointed to prosper. My eyes are open to see creative ways to increase financially; my ears are open to hear the best deals, and my heart is pure so that you can channel finances through me. I am on the path of perpetual increase as I enter my wealthy place! Wealth & riches are in my house. I declare that I am the righteousness of God. I've sown my seed for supernatural abundance, and I live in a daily expectation of increase. Money comes to me; my nature attracts money. The fear of lack has been broken. I free from debt! I am the lender and not the borrower! The wealth of the wicked is being transferred to me. I thank you for daily you are loading me with benefits. You want to increase me more and more. Abundance is your will for me! I call increase, abundance and prosperity to come to me now! And I will never be broke another day in my life!"

Reflective Thoughts:

-E-
EMOTIONAL INTELLIGENCE

Everyone is equipped with intelligence to some degree. Intelligence is an all-encompassing thing. It's not just about how much knowledge you have and how well you are able to use that knowledge, but it is also about how emotionally intelligent you are. Emotional intelligence is the capacity to be aware of, control, and express one's emotions, and to handle interpersonal relationships judiciously and empathetically. When it comes to reaching certain levels of success or happiness in your life your Emotional Quotient or EQ is just as important as your Intelligence Quotient or IQ. Much of our interactions and how far we advance in life has to do with our level of emotional intelligence. The good news is that you can improve your emotional intelligence. Like with anything worth having, you must practice and exercise it regularly to increase it. Remember it starts with YOU!

Having emotional intelligence can help relieve many people from hostile or challenging situations in life. You can't control other people and their behaviors towards you. However, you can control your emotions and your responses to other people, which in turn has certain influential effect on other people and the situation at hand. When faced with situations that you need to invoke self-control always center yourself first. There's a reason the airline attendants tell you to secure your own mask first. It's because of a condition called hypoxia that occurs at very high altitudes when there is a loss of oxygen and you can very quickly lose control of your own motor skills, and eventually consciousness. It happens in a matter of minutes. So, you must ensure that your mask is on first before helping little Timmy sitting next to you, because by the time you have regulated your oxygen levels little Timmy is passed out because you put his mask on his ear instead of his mouth! All due to your hypoxia, causing your inability to help. Instead, you can cause more harm. All of that to say that you should always center yourself before responding to challenging situations. Use your emotional intelligence to have self-awareness and self-control.

According to Daniel Goldman, there are five key elements to emotional intelligence:

- **Self-Awareness**- Consciousness knowledge of one's own character, feelings, motives, and desires.
- **Self-Regulation**- The fact of a person or entity being able to regulate itself without intervention from external sources.
- **Motivation**- an explanation of why people initiate, continue, or terminate certain behaviors at times

- **Empathy**- Understanding another person's experience by imagining oneself in that other person's situation, being able to sense their emotions.

- **Social Skills**- The skills we use every day to communicate with others. These include verbal & non-verbal communication, such as speech, gestures, facial expressions, and body language.

In many ways I feel the instructions that Peter gave in the bible, he was trying to help the people increase their emotional intelligence. *"... Supplement your faith with a generous provision of moral excellence, and moral excellence with knowledge, and knowledge with self-control, and self- control with patient endurance, and patient endurance with godliness, and godliness with brotherly affection, and brotherly affection with love for everyone." 2 Peter 1:5-7, NLT*

List some ways or areas that you can practice self-awareness and self-control.

1_____

2. _____

3. _____

4._____

5._____

6._____

Reflective Thoughts:

-F-
FOCUS

I'll be the first to admit that it's increasingly hard for me to stay focused these days. I constantly have to repeat one of my many mantras to myself daily which is, "Focus on yourself, sis!" When I repeat this mantra it not only serves as a reminder to worry about myself and what I have going on but it also automatically puts me into "grind mode". I automatically get back to whatever it was I was doing. Not sure if my onset of Adult ADD (attention deficit disorder) is hereditary, environmental, or circumstantial. ADD, also sometimes referred to as ADHD (attention deficit hyperactivity disorder) is a neuro-developmental disorder that occurs in children, teens, and adults. The core symptoms are Inattention, Impulsivity, and Hyperactivity. If you experience any of these symptoms on a regular basis then you could be experiencing Adult ADD or ADHD as well!

A few things that help me regain focus or manage my Adult ADD are:

1. Setting my phone aside on DND
2. Breaking up my tasks into small chunks throughout the day to avoid my brain feeling fried

3. Taking multiple mini breaks throughout the day where I don't have to "think" but I can just zone out

4. Play music!

I don't take any supplements or anything to help me focus, but I know they exist. So, if you need to investigate that go ahead! There are prescriptions and natural supplements as well, to each their own! Do not feel ashamed if you need substances to assist you with focusing or managing ADD or ADHD

List some practices that you will commit to including in your routine to help you focus.

_____

_____

_____

_____

_____

_____

_____

_____

_____

_____

_____

_____

_____

_____

Reflective Thoughts:

-G-
GRATITUDE

G ratitude is the quality of being thankful and having the readiness to express appreciation. I spend most of my day expressing gratitude as a habit. It has become second nature for me now to give thanks by simply saying "thank you".

It's one of the first things I utter each morning and usually the last before bed. Positive Psychologists suggest that the practice of expressing gratitude is consistently associated with having greater happiness in your life. Expressing gratitude can also help with increasing your overall health, being able to cherish good times, building stronger relationships, and dealing with adversity better.

There are several ways to express gratitude. The easiest and quickest way is verbal. Other ways include smiling, helping others, cleaning your space, writing letters, lists, or keeping a journal. Taking time to do any or all these things shows your care and appreciation, and helps you express gratitude even when you're not sure how to.

"Rejoice always, pray without ceasing, *in everything give thanks*; for this is the will of God in Christ Jesus for you." 1 Thessalonians 5:16-18 NKJV

What are some ways that you express gratitude?

_____

_____

_____

_____

_____

_____

_____

_____

_____

_____

Reflective Thoughts:

-H-
HEALTH

O verall Health is important! Not just physical health, but mental, social, and spiritual health are a part of your overall health and well-being.

If you're the type of person who only focuses on your physical body being in shape and taken care of but you neglect your emotions or your spiritual needs, then I hate to break it to you but... You're NOT healthy.

According to research, there are five main aspects to optimal health: physical, emotional, social, spiritual, and intellectual.

It's important to incorporate practices in each area that will help you be healthier.

I know you can do it!

"Beloved, I pray that you may prosper in all things and be in health, just as your soul prospers" 3 John 1:2 NKJV

Below are some practices that you can start now to become healthier in each of these areas. You task is to list at least one additional thing you will commit to in each area below that will help you reach optimal health.

To improve my *physical health,* I can commit to move or exercise my body at least 3 times per week for at least 30 minutes.

I will also:

_____

_____

_____

To improve my *emotional health,* I will avoid people or situations who trigger negative feelings.

I will also:

_____

_____

_____

To improve my *social health,* I will practice active listening while in social settings.

I will also:

_____

_____

To improve my **spiritual health,** I will practice prayer or meditation more often during the week.

I will also:

_____

_____

To improve my **intellectual health,** I will read more books or articles that teach me something new.

I will also:

_____

_____

Reflective Thoughts:

-I-
INTENTIONS

How often do you set intentions? Setting intentions is the act of stating what you intend to accomplish through your actions. It's a lot like planning, but less about the what and how of things and more focused on the *why.* When you can clearly figure out why you want to do something then it helps you set intentions better because you will have a clearer motive for your actions. Then all your plans will help your intentions realize.

If you never set intentions (figure out your motive) and instead just do things "on the fly" or without much thought, then your actions could garner some serious repercussions. Not just for you but for others as well! All because you weren't intentional. Yes, sometimes it's ok to not have a "plan" per se... but you should still be mindful of your motives and reasons for doing anything, which will help you achieve the desired results.

Setting intentions is activating a part of your own receptivity because whatever you give out is what you will end up receiving. We should do nothing without intention God was very intentional when he created us!

"I knew you before I formed you in your mother's womb. Before you were born, I set you apart..." {redacted} Jeremiah 1:5 NLT
"For I know the plans I have for you," declares the Lord, "plans to prosper you and not to harm, plans to give you hope and a future" Jeremiah 29:11 NIV

Practice setting intentions as you plan the activities of your day. Really think about what it is you want to accomplish, and the impact you want to have.

What do you want to accomplish? How can you be more intentional with your actions?

_____

_____

_____

_____

_____

_____

_____

_____

_____

_____

To understand your motives now ask yourself *why* you want to accomplish these things. Who will they benefit?

_____

_____

_____

_____

_____

_____

Now, you can set forth a plan which includes steps, action items, or key behaviors to incorporate that will help you reach your accomplishments by understanding your motives.

Reflective Thoughts:

-J-
JOY

Do you know the difference between happiness and joy? Joy is consistent and cultivated internally. It's a more intrinsic state of being. It comes when you have made peace with who you are, why you are, and how you are. Whereas happiness tends to be more externally motivated, based on people, places, things, or events that happened to you. Having joy doesn't mean that you won't ever experience hardships, disappointments, heartbreaks, or problems. Having joy just means that regardless of what happens to you, you'll be able to look at those unpleasant situations and find the lessons or growth opportunities of them.

We are instructed in the Bible by James to count our troubles of any kind as growth opportunities. Because from those troubles can come great joy!

"Dear brothers and sisters, when troubles of any kind come your way, consider it an opportunity for great joy. For you know that when your faith is tested, your endurance has a chance to grow. So let it grow" James 1:2-4 NLT

I have practices that help cultivate joy in my life such as prayer, gratitude, travel, meditation, journaling, expressing appreciation for moments and people in my life.

What types of things can you do to help cultivate joy in your life?

_____

_____

_____

_____

_____

_____

_____

Reflective Thoughts:

_____

_____

_____

_____

_____

_____

_____

_____

_____

_____

_____

_____

_____

_____

_____

_____

_____

_____

_____

_____

_____

_____

_____

-K-
KARMA

Bottom line…" what goes around, comes around" is more than just a cliche statement. It's facts, law, science, and even in the Bible! I know that the word "karma" doesn't always sit well with folk, but it doesn't exempt you from being a recipient of karma based on the intentions, deeds, and actions that you put out. So, it's simple if you want to be good both now and, in the future, then you should do good.

"Do not be deceived, God is not mocked for whatever a man sows that will he also reap." Galatians 6:7 NKJV

What can you do today to plant seeds of good karma for yourself?

_____

_____

_____

_____

_____

_____

_____

Reflective Thoughts:

-L-
LEADERSHIP

L eadership is defined as the action of leading a group of people or an organization. Not to be confused with "management". Tasks, processes, and systems require management. People often need leadership. Leaders don't have to necessarily be appointed, but sometimes the leadership role is taken on based on the level of influence they may have on others. A good leader will always put the needs of the people they serve first. They will listen to them, they make sure develop their people and help push them to become better. Leaders know that if they aren't equipping others to dream, do, learn, and become better than their role as a leader is useless.

Take a few moments and think about who you may be a leader for. It could be anyone you are responsible for or have influence over.

List their names:

_____

_____

_____

Now think about what you can do as a leader to help develop them.

_____

_____

_____

_____

_____

_____

_____

Reflective Thoughts:

-M-
MINDSET

C hange starts in the brain! That's right... Your mind and thoughts control your behavior and actions and therefore have an impact on your life. So many people claim they want better for themselves but aren't sure where to start and it's simple! It starts with your mindset and how you think. Your mindset is essentially your belief system. It's made up of assumptions, practices, notions, and methods. Having a growth mindset allows you to think about possibilities and opportunities. On the opposite end, a fixed mindset only allows you to think about what you can see, or the options in front of you. If you really want to change your life, start to adopt a different idea about the things you want to change.

For example, you may have a job that you're not too happy with and really want to start a new job in a new field. Well, having a fixed mindset will keep you there forever. Here are a few thoughts that someone with a fixed mindset may have in this situation:

I want to start a new job:" I *don't have the skills to apply for this job.*" "*I don't know anyone who does this job*", or "*they would never hire me because I am not qualified for this job*"

These statements reflect a fixed mindset. Below I want you to write out a contrasting statement to each of these that reflect a growth mindset.

Instead of *"I don't have the skills to apply for this job"*
A growth mindset statement would be:

_____

Instead of *"I don't know anyone who does this job"*
A growth mindset statement would be:

_____

Instead of *"They will never hire me because I am not qualified for this job"*
A growth mindset statement would be:

_____

Now that you have practiced thinking through contrasting statements that help move you from a fixed mindset to a growth mindset, adopt this practice with everything that you do. Your life will change!

"Jesus said to him, "If you can believe, all things are possible to him who believes" Mark 9:23 NKJV

Reflective Thoughts:

-N-
NOBLE

Nobility is honorable. Have you ever met someone who you know does good for others and is genuinely interested in doing things for the greater good? Nobility is having or showing fine personal qualities, or high morals and ideals. Think about someone who you hold in high regard. Someone who is selfless and has a mission to make a difference or positive impact in the world but done with humility. I feel this way about the Obama's.

On the contrary we've all met people who seemingly do things just for clout or recognition & reward. Those people are narcissists. A noble person will do those same good deeds without seeking any praise or recognition. They do it because they want to make an impact in the world and in the lives of others. The world could use more nobles and less narcissists.

"Who is wise and understanding among you? Let them show it by their good life, by deeds done in the humility that comes from wisdom" James 3:13 NIV

In what ways can you practice more nobility?

_____

_____

_____

_____

_____

_____

_____

_____

Reflective Thoughts:

-O-
OPEN

We've been doing a lot of work on ourselves. Growing & glowing, doing inner healing work, journaling, releasing things that no longer serve us, and overall trying to manifest our dreams! However, there's still work to be done on remaining open to what God actually has for us. I'm guilty of this too: praying for something, trusting I'll receive it, visualize it, then something presents itself and I realize I may not be as open to that particular thing. Why is this? Is it cultural, or are we conditioned to be skeptical? I'm not sure of the answer but I do believe that in order for us to get what God has for us we got to open our hearts, minds, and eyes to things that we may not normally go after or accept!

Ephesians 3:20 tells us that he can do exceedingly more than we could even imagine! So, for us to receive that we must remain open to receive. We can't think in a closed-minded, judgmental way when we are asking God for miracles! We forget that God can do anything and can use anyone because everything in the universe belongs to him!

Let's practice not shooting down things when they come just because they do fit into our small mind's frame of thinking. What are some areas that you can be more open and accepting in?

i.e., "I can be open to talking to people who are not like me. Perhaps they can be the catalyst to my next blessing" or "I can go places that I haven't been before to experience new things"

"Now to him who is able to do immeasurably more than all we ask or imagine, according tohis power that is at work within us, to Him be all glory in the church and in Christ Jesus throughout all generations, forever and ever! Amen" Ephesians 3:20 NIV

List some things that you are going to be more open to below:

_____

_____

_____

_____

_____

_____

_____

_____

_____

_____

_____

Reflective Thoughts:

-P-
PATIENCE

Patience is a virtue" we've all heard this before. Some of us have more patience than others. At varying times in life, we may have little or more patience than usual. What drives patience? I've found that it's dependent on how content I am with my current situation or how busy I am. When I am content with what I may currently have then I'm okay to wait for something better. This can be applied to any situation. For example, if I've ordered food on uber eats let's say, I'm usually pretty patient if I'm not starving or experiencing hunger pangs. But if I am experiencing any hunger pangs then I might not be as patient to wait for the food to be delivered, so I'll choose a quicker option. Perhaps this is why restaurants serve appetizers before the main course entree? Appetizers are meant to be served quickly and be small enough to satisfy your hunger while you wait for the main dish to be served. Another way for me to exercise patience is if I'm not focused on whatever it is I'm waiting for. So, I'll place my order and then I'll get busy with something else. Whether it's work or cleaning, etc. Something to occupy my time and focus causing me to have more patience.

This is the same thing that happens when I'm waiting on things I've been trying to manifest. The way for me to remain patient is to not be focused on the things I'm waiting on, but instead, get busy working on what I have in front of me. There is always something to be done. So if I'm distracted, or my focus is elsewhere then I can exercise patience and before I know it, I will have what I've been waiting for!

The key is to stay focused and busy! When we don't have anything to occupy our time and attention, we become desperate, and we become impatient. Being impatient isn't going to make your manifestations come in any sooner. In fact, you'll just be tormenting yourself. So, when you find your patience running thin, my advice to you is to find something to do!

"Yet I am confident I will see the Lord's goodness while I am here in the land of the living. Wait patiently for the Lord. Be brave and courageous. Yes, wait patiently for the Lord" Psalms 27:13-14 NLT

List some things below that could use your attention and focus while you are patiently waiting for the things you are trying to manifest?

_____

_____

_____

_____

_____

_____

_____

_____

_____

_____

_____

_____

_____

Reflective Thoughts:

_____

_____

_____

_____

_____

_____

_____

_____

_____

_____

_____

_____

_____

_____

_____

_____

_____

_____

_____

_____

_____

-Q-
QUIRKS

Have you ever been called weird or awkward because of certain quirks you may have? Are You embarrassed by those quirks? Those little idiosyncrasies are what make us unique! They are what makes you, YOU. Unless your quirks are a danger to yourself or others, embrace them! Embrace those things that make you different and don't let anyone make you feel bad for having them. When God made you, he was intentional. Quirks are just unusual or peculiar characteristics. But that was on purpose!

"But ye are a chosen generation, a royal priesthood, a holy nation, a peculiar people... "{redacted} 1 Peter 2:9 KJV

Take a moment to list out all the things that you think make you special or unique. **What are some characteristics that you have that you haven't been able to identify in your close friend group or family members yet?** Those unidentifiable things are what make you special. So, embrace them!

_____

_____

_____

_____

_____

_____

_____

_____

_____

_____

_____

_____

_____

Now list how you can use those quirks for good or add value to the environments that you frequent

_____

_____

_____

_____

_____

_____

_____

_____

_____

Reflective Thoughts:

-R-
RESPONSIBILITY

I've heard the term responsibility broken down like this…Your ability to respond to certain situations gives you responsibility however that doesn't equal ownership. Just because you can respond to a situation doesn't mean you always should. We often take on problems that aren't ours because we use our ability to respond. When should we use our ability to respond? If you're the one suffering or being impacted by the issue, then it's your problem and you should use your ability to respond. In other words, it's your responsibility! When you don't respond appropriately to a situation then you become the victim. Don't be a victim of circumstance. James 4:17 tells us that whoever knows the right things and fails to do it, for him it is sin.

Take responsibility for those things that you can and should! That's how you remain a winner and not a victim. You are responsible and should respond accordingly to things that require your attention because they have an impact in your life.

Take a moment to list out those things that require your attention and that you can respond to. Then list out the options you have to make those things happen. If something is out of your control then don't stress over it, but if there is something you can do then list those options out.

Things that Require My Attention	Plan of Action
_____	_____
_____	_____
_____	_____
_____	_____
_____	_____
_____	_____
_____	_____
_____	_____
_____	_____
_____	_____
_____	_____

Reflective Thoughts:

-S-
STOICISM

I would consider myself a very emotional person. Not because I'm overly emotional but because I understand my emotions and how to control them. Just because I have them doesn't mean I'm controlled by them. I've learned over the years that emotions are valid and necessary and normal. However, I don't think it's wise to make sound decisions while being emotional. There is a certain level of stoicism that one should have to make a sound decision versus an emotional one which could cost you later down the line. Stoicism is described as the endurance of pain or hardship without the display of feelings and without complaint.

Please don't get me wrong, I'm not saying to ignore your pain or hardship. In fact, you should embrace those times. You'll eventually emerge a stronger person having gone through hardship and making it out of hardship. But I'm admonishing you not to make any major decisions while in pain. Unless the decision is to get help for your distress. But making an emotional decision can lead to a decision that you'll probably end up regretting later.

The Bible tells us to make decisions with a sound mind since that is the mind of Christ. *"Let this mind be in you, which was also in Christ Jesus." Philippians 2:5 NKJV*

When Jesus was emotionally dealing with his impending death, he didn't make any decisions, instead, he went up to the garden to pray. Then once his mind was clear he knew what was required of him.

"God has not given us the spirit of fear (an emotion), but of power, and of love and of a sound mind!" 2 Timothy 1:7 KJV

When you are feeling overwhelmed with emotions, take a moment to first stop. Next, feel your emotions whatever they may be. Cry, pray, scream, do whatever is necessary to get those emotions out. Then once you are relaxed and calmer, use your sound mind and your ability to respond to make a sound decision. Invoke your stoicism.

What situation are you currently being overly emotional about?

_____

_____

_____

_____

Which emotion do you need to remove from the situation?

_____

_____

_____

_____

_____

What is a practical step you can take to help move you closer to a resolution?

_____

_____

_____

_____

_____

Reflective Thoughts:

-T-
THOUGHTFUL

How thoughtful are you? No seriously, do you put thought into the things that you do or say, or do you operate on autopilot? Thoughtfulness is evident. You can tell when someone has put thought into things, even things as simple as a well-put-together outfit, or a well-thought-out gift for someone. It's easy to get into our "zone" and operate and do things out of habit but I want to encourage you to be more intentional and thoughtful in everything that you do today. Make thoughtful decisions, think through possibilities and options, and take your time making choices. I promise you when you put more thought into things, you will feel a certain sense of accomplishment and pride. You will be able to make choices that you are proud of and that stand out to others. God was very thoughtful with you.

"For I know the plans I have for you, declares the Lord, plans to prosper you and not to harm you, plans to give you hope and a future." Jeremiah 29:11 NIV

Here are a few small things you can put more thought into today to practice being thoughtful.

- What do you want for breakfast?
- How do you want it prepared?
- Is there anyone else in the house with you that may also want breakfast?
- Do you know what they like and how they may like it?
- What's on your agenda for the day?
- Are you going out or staying in?
- What is the temperature or expected weather?
- Are there any special events happening at work, or home, or otherwise?
- How should you dress?

I know these just seem like a lot of questions, but considering these things helps you to plan. The purpose of asking these questions isn't to cause stress of obsession over anything. But it helps to think through details like this to become more thoughtful.

Even if things don't go as planned, you'll still feel better having considered these things that you may have overlooked before.

Reflective Thoughts:

-U-
UNDERSTANDING

"Wisdom is the principal thing; Therefore, get wisdom. And in all your getting, get understanding" Proverbs 4:7 NKJV

When we are curious about a topic, we seek out knowledge and information to understand that topic better. This is true for everything. Sometimes we find ourselves in situations where we need more clarity. Some may even call it closure. But I believe what we are truly seeking is understanding in those moments. Although there may be times where we are still left wondering or confused about something, I think the key here is to be open to and make an effort to seek out understanding. At least when you try to get an understanding, then you can say you have done your part. The next time you have a disagreement with someone, instead of trying to make your point or get one across to them, seek to understand what they are communicating to you. Whether it be through their actions or words, seek understanding, which may mean you'll have to ask for it.

What or who can you commit to gaining a better understanding of?

_____

_____

_____

_____

_____

_____

_____

_____

_____

_____

Reflective Thoughts:

-V-
VISION

How do you envision your life? Do you ever stop to visualize a reality that doesn't mirror your current reality? If not, you need to start today!

"Where these is no vision, the people perish…"

Proverbs 29:18 KJV

It's important to understand the difference between having vision versus having sight. Sight just means you can see. It's usually whatever is in front of you at that moment. But sometimes what we see isn't our destiny. Our vision determines our destiny! A person with a vision doesn't look at the current, they look towards the future! But just like it tells us in Proverbs, without that vision you will perish. Fail. Be stuck. Sometimes we have visions involuntarily, through dreams at night. I don't know about you, but I have very vivid dreams. I always have, since I was a child. And guess what, sometimes my dreams would happen! Sometimes it was scary and sometimes amazing! But what it taught me was that dreams may not always be far from our possibly reality. That's when I discovered the power of visualization. If all I had to do was dream it or visualize it then I could make it happen. Our minds are just powerful like that.

Let's practice visualization. In a moment you will close your eyes and think about the life you *want* to live. Consider each question below then close your eyes to envision it for a few moments (set a time if you must) before writing your answer. Relish in those visions. Don't limit yourself. Imagine the best life you could for yourself. Nothing is off limits.

How do you look?

_____

_____

Where are you?

_____

_____

Who is around you?

_____

_____

How do you feel?

_____

_____

You must see it before you live it! Once you have your vision intact, then you should follow up by speaking those things as though they already are! Practice visualizing your life until the things you envisioned are what you actually see. I can't wait to hear your testimonies!

Reflective Thoughts:

Conclusion

Congratulations! You have successfully completed your A thru V journey! I'm so grateful and thankful that you decided to go on this journey with me. Thank you for allowing me to impact your life! I really want this to be the beginning of your fulfilled life. I hope to learn how this journal helped you. Please don't hesitate to contact me via my socials to provide feedback on how this journal impacted you.

I hope it was practical enough for you to use and reference repeatedly. The final task for you will be to share it with someone that you want to have an impact on. I'm sure they will be so grateful!

Wishing you abundant blessings!

VICTORIA NJIDEKA
Host of The V List Podcast

Reflective Thoughts:

Reflective Thoughts:

Reflective Thoughts:

Reflective Thoughts:

Reflective Thoughts:

Reflective Thoughts:

_____

_____

_____

_____

_____

_____

_____

_____

_____

_____

_____

_____

_____

_____

_____

_____

_____

_____

_____

Reflective Thoughts:

Reflective Thoughts:

Reflective Thoughts:

Reflective Thoughts:

Reflective Thoughts:

Reflective Thoughts:

VICTORIA NJIDEKA

Reflective Thoughts:

Reflective Thoughts:

Reflective Thoughts: